FIND OUT ABOUT

THE
UNITED
KINGDOM

Where is the UK?

The United Kingdom (UK) is an island that lies off the northwest coast of mainland Europe. There are four countries in the UK: England, Scotland, Wales, and Northern Ireland. England, Scotland, and Wales all make up Britain, and Northern Ireland lies to the west, across the Irish Sea.

The UK is separated from Europe by the English Channel, although a tunnel under the sea links England to France and it's possible to travel through the tunnel by train or by car. Ferries also make very frequent crossings to France, Spain, Belgium, and the Netherlands.

Hello, I'm Kate and I'll see you later for a trip around the UK.

In this book you'll find out about not just the United Kingdom but also the different customs and accents in England, Scotland, Wales, and Northern Ireland. The Taylor family will guide you round Britain. They live in Leicester, in central England, and although Mr. Taylor is English, his wife is Scottish. They have two children: Jack, aged nine, and Kate, ten.

2

 Follow this book bar for helpful hints and top tips about exploring the UK.

Five flags

The flag of the United Kingdom is the Union Flag (known as the Union Jack when it's flown at sea), but each country also has its own flag.

The Union Flag is a combination of the national flags of Scotland and England.

England
National flower: rose
Patron saint: Saint George

Scotland
National flower: thistle
Patron saint: Saint Andrew

Northern Ireland
National flower: shamrock
Patron saint: Saint Patrick

Wales
National flower: daffodil
Patron saint: Saint David

h the internet to discover the other emblem of Wales.

The Orkney Islands lie ten miles north of the Scottish mainland and the Shetland Isles are 100 miles north.

The Isle of Wight lies in the English Channel five miles off the south coast of England.

Cairngorm Mountains

Glasgow

Edinburgh

Stranraer

Lake District

Belfast

Manchester

Liverpool

Snowdonia

Leicester

Cardiff

London

Stonehenge

Dover

The Scilly Isles are also part of the UK – find out more at www.simplyscilly.co.uk

An introduction to the UK

Just over 60 million people live in the United Kingdom, which makes it one of the most densely populated countries in the world. That's because the UK isn't very big; from the most northerly point to the most southerly, it is about 600 miles and just under 300 miles at its widest point.

Because of its long and rich history, the United Kingdom is a fascinating country to visit, and no matter where you go you will see evidence of the past, from ancient monasteries to medieval castles to grand palaces. You can even walk across battlefields where 1,000 years ago soldiers fought with swords and spears!

And if after all your sightseeing you need a rest, there are hundreds of museums and theaters and sports stadiums where you can discover more about the United Kingdom and its people.

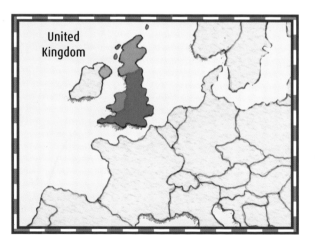

United Kingdom

■ Scotland
■ England
■ Northern Ireland
■ Wales

The position of the UK within Europe.

Mother tongue

English is the language spoken in the United Kingdom, and it derives from Old English, which was a mixture of different languages.

The English language contains many words that were introduced by the Normans and the Vikings over 1,000 years ago.

As well as English, there are also some other languages spoken in the UK. Look at the people below and try to guess what they are all saying.

English	Old Norse
gun	gunnhildr
mistake	mistaka
weird	wyrd

English	Norman
candle	aundèle
garden	gardîn
captain	capitain

In Northern Ireland some people also speak Irish.

The Cornish language has recently been revived.

Gaelic is spoken in the north of Scotland.

About 20 percent of Welsh people speak Welsh.

Dia dhuit!

Dydh da!

Halò!

Bore da!

That's right, they're all saying "hello" to you!

Introduction

It's time to take a closer look at the United Kingdom!

Did you know?

👍 The motto of the British monarchy is "Dieu et mon droit," which is French for "God and my right."

👍 More people live in London than in any other European city.

👍 The Queen is head of state in the United Kingdom, and the prime minister is head of government.

👍 The airport at Belfast is named after the famous Northern Ireland soccer star, George Best.

👍 Cardiff was proclaimed capital of Wales in 1955.

👍 The population of the United Kingdom is just over 60 million, making it the 22nd most populous country in the world.

👍 In 1888, Queen Victoria granted Belfast its city status.

👍 The tallest building in the UK (2008) is One Canada Square in London's Canary Wharf. It is 771 ft. high.

👍 London is one of the three major financial centers in the world.

👍 Cars drive on the left of the road in the UK because hundreds of years ago, horsemen rode on the left so they would have their right arm free to fight if they were attacked by outlaws.

A journey around the UK

The 66 cities in the United Kingdom are linked by a network of trains, planes, and highways. Did you know, for example, that there are over 2,000 miles of motorways and a further 29,145 miles of main roads?

Then there is the UK's rail system, which is the oldest in the world. George Stephenson built the first locomotive to be successfully powered by steam. He became the chief engineer for several railways, including the the world's first intercity rail network running between Liverpool and Manchester in 1830. At one time the UK rail system consisted of 30,000 miles of tracks, but today that figure has been reduced to 10,200 miles. It takes 24 hours to travel from Penzance, Cornwall, the most southerly rail station, to Thurso in the far north of Scotland. But what a journey! On your way you'll go through forests, around lakes, and over mountains.

It takes less than two hours to fly from London to the Shetland Islands.

England

England is by far the biggest country in the UK and with 50 million people contains 83 percent of the UK population. The weather in the south of England is better than anywhere else in the UK, and beaches in Cornwall, Devon, and Dorset are very popular.

Sherlock Holmes

There are no mountains in the south, but the land can be wild and rugged nonetheless. Dartmoor in the southwest was the setting for the famous Sherlock Holmes book *The Hound of the Baskervilles*. The further north you go in England, the more hills you'll find. The highest peak is in the Lake District, the 3,200 ft. Scafell Pike. The largest lake is Windermere at 10.5 miles long and 200 ft. deep.

But no matter where you go in England, you'll find wonderful old castles, stately homes, and pretty little villages—and if you go in the summer you might even catch a game of village cricket!

The Lake District

Bodiam Castle in Sussex

Cricket on the village green

6

Scotland

A word of warning: Scots don't wear kilts and play the bagpipes every day! The kilt is worn on special occasions such as weddings and birthday parties.

A Scottish wedding

Scotland is known for its mountains, forests, lochs, and glens, not to mention the nearly 800 small islands that lie off its coastline. Some of these islands, like beautiful Skye, have a population of several thousand, but many are uninhabited except for wildlife.

It can get very cold in Scotland, and during the winter skiing is popular in the Highlands. Although it doesn't get as warm as it does in the south of England, Scotland is beautiful when the summer sun shines and you can go swimming in some of the many rivers and lochs.

The farming, fishing, and oil industries are very important for Scotland and to the five million people who live there.

More than a million puffins come every year

The Red deer is a symbol of Scotland

Visit www.visitscotland.com to find out more about Scotland.

Wales

Three million people live in Wales, which is about one-quarter the size of Scotland. In the north of the country is the breathtaking National Park of Snowdonia as well as the seaside resorts of Rhyl and Llandudno. But the best beaches are further south, along the Pembrokeshire coastline and on the Gower Peninsula.

The Gower Peninsula

For centuries Wales was famous for its mines, such as coal, iron, and lead, but that is no longer the case. Instead, cattle and sheep farming have become very important, and so has tourism, with millions visiting each year to climb the mountains, canoe the rivers, and walk the coastlines.

The national sport is rugby union and most towns have a team that is always loudly supported whenever it plays.

Making a rugby tackle

8

Northern Ireland

Northern Ireland is the smallest of the four countries in the UK with a population of around 1.7 million. The capital city is Belfast and the name means "mouth of the river." Northern Ireland is made up of six counties—Antrim, Armagh, Down, Fermanagh, Londonderry, and Tyrone—all with a reputation for beautiful rolling green countryside. It boasts the biggest freshwater lake in the UK, Lough Neagh, which covers 151 square miles and is popular with anglers and bird watchers. It's also famous for eels, a Northern Irish delicacy.

The Mountains of Mourne are in the southeast corner, and the summit of Slieve Donard provides stunning views. The coast was once well-known for smuggling.

Agriculture is important, with sheep and cattle being raised for their meat, and a wide variety of crops grown.

Bird watching

Cranes from the Northern Irish shipbuilding industry

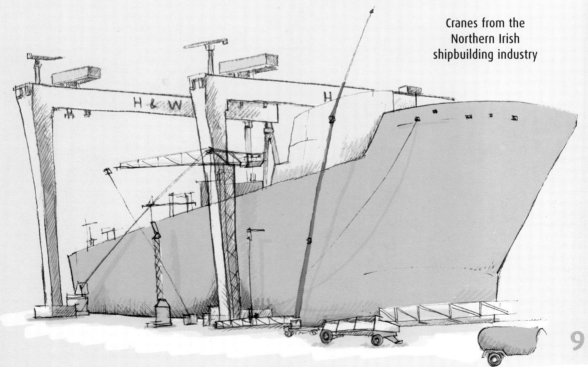

9

London and the big cities

The Romans first built a settlement on the River Thames in 43 A.D. and called it Londinium. Nearly 2,000 years later over seven million people live in Greater London, and it is one of the best known cities in the world.

London is famous for many things, such as its green parks, its black cabs, its red double-decker buses, the statue of Nelson in Trafalgar Square and, of course, the River Thames. But London is best known for its many historic buildings such as the Tower of London, Big Ben, and Buckingham Palace, where the Queen lives with her corgi dogs!

Trafalgar Square

London Eye

Tower Bridge

Big Ben

10

Search the internet to find out where the River Thames starts and finishes!

Edinburgh

The rock on which Edinburgh Castle stands is believed to have been inhabited from at least 850 B.C. Today nearly half a million people live in Edinburgh, and it is the second most popular tourist destination in Britain. Although Scotland is part of the United Kingdom, the country has its own parliament and its modern building is well worth visiting.

Edinburgh Castle

Glasgow

Although Edinburgh is the capital city of Scotland, more people live and work in Glasgow, which is 40 miles west. Glasgow was built 1,500 years ago on the banks of the River Clyde, and the city was once famous for making great ships and for transatlantic trade with the Americas. Soccer is very popular, and there is traditional rivalry between the city's two main clubs. The soccer stadium, Hampden Park, is very modern and is home to Scotland's national football team.

Hampden Park Stadium

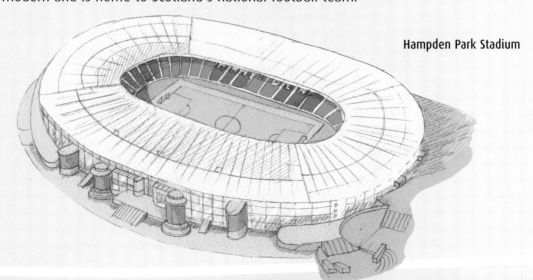

11

What are the names of the two big soccer clubs in Glasgow?

Belfast

Belfast was an important port for years, particularly when the linen trade flourished in the 18th and 19th centuries. It once had the largest shipyard in the world. The city's prosperity declined in the 20th century, not helped by the years of conflict between the Roman Catholic and Protestant communities. However, since the Good Friday Agreement of 1998, Belfast has seen a boom in development, and more tourists are visiting each year to enjoy the famous Irish hospitality! The Northern Ireland politicians sit at Stormont Parliament Buildings.

Stormont Parliament Buildings

Cardiff

The Romans first built a fort in Cardiff nearly 2,000 years ago, but it wasn't until the Normans invaded Britain in 1066 that a town began to emerge. In the 19th century, coal from the Welsh mines was exported. Although the coal mining industry has all but died now, Cardiff has turned the old docks into dazzling new office blocks, shops, and cafés. And, of course, right in the heart of the city is the Millennium Stadium—where 75,000 fans can cheer on the Welsh rugby team when they play!

Millennium Stadium

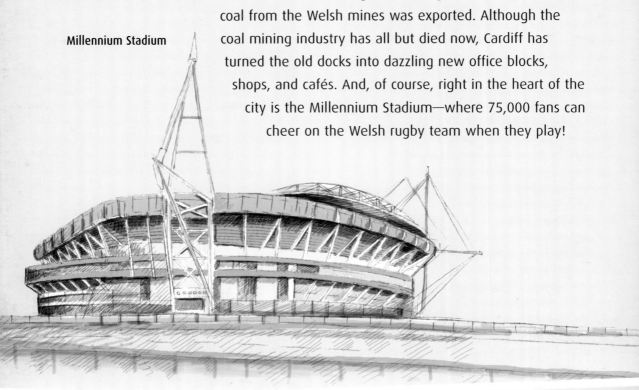

Find out more about the Wales rugby team by visiting www.wru.co.uk

Life in the UK

part two

It's interesting to learn about how people live in other countries.

Did you know?

👍 Each year, Highland Games are held in Scotland, with events such as putting the stone and tossing the caber.

👍 There is no British soccer or cricket team but Irish, Welsh, and Scottish players have all played for the England cricket team.

👍 The King's School in Canterbury, England, was founded in the year 597.

👍 The biggest sports stadium in the UK is Wembley in London, home of the England soccer team. It can hold 90,000 fans.

👍 All children must attend school from the age of six to fifteen.

👍 Although the kilt is usually associated with Scotland, there is also an Irish and a Welsh kilt.

👍 England won the Rugby World Cup in 2003 and were the runners-up in 2007.

👍 A version of baseball is played in Wales with the pitcher throwing the ball underhand instead of overhand.

👍 Many sports were invented in the UK, including football, rugby, cricket, tennis, and golf.

👍 In 1872 Scotland became the first country in the UK in which children had to go to school.

Meet the family

Say "hello" to the Taylor family. They are going to be your guides around the United Kingdom and will help you learn about the lives of the people.

I'm Mr. Taylor, and I was born in England.

I'm Mrs. Taylor, and I was born in Scotland.

I'm Kate, and I can't wait to show you around!

I'm Jack, and I'm happy you want to find out about the UK.

Like many families in the United Kingdom, the Taylors are a mix of the four countries. Mrs. Taylor is Scottish and was born in Glasgow, but moved to England to work and married Mr. Taylor. One of Mr. Taylor's sisters married a Welshman and lives in Cardiff. His brother lives in Belfast with his Northern Irish wife. What a mixture of accents there are at family reunions!

13

They will tell you about life in the UK—at home, at school, and having fun.

At school

Kate and Jack go to a primary school in Leicester that is for boys and girls between five and eleven years old. Like most schoolchildren in the United Kingdom, Kate and Jack wear a school uniform.

At Kate and Jack's school, girls and boys wear a blue tie with a blue v-necked sweater that has the school badge on it.

Kate wears a grey skirt and black shoes, and Jack wears grey trousers with black shoes. Sometimes Jack wears shorts, but only when it's warm, because otherwise his knees knock together with the cold!

When you're done with classes at 3:30 I'll meet you right here.

Great! You can walk with me to my swimming lesson.

14

 Kate and Jack live near their school, so they can walk there together.

There is school every day of the week in the UK, but not on the weekend. Lessons start at Kate and Jack's school at 9 A.M. and at 10:30 they have a break for half an hour. Jack and his friends play football in the playground; Kate and her friends play hopscotch.

Lunchtime lasts from 12 noon to 1 P.M. and many children eat packed lunches that they bring from home.

Lessons in the afternoon last until 3:30 P.M. and include math, computing, spelling, art, and PE. Jack often comes home with a scrape on his knee because he's fallen over!

Vaulting the horse is awesome! I wish we had PE every day!

There's lots to do in the gym, and PE is Jack's favorite lesson.

After school

Like children around the world, Kate and Jack can't wait for school to finish! There are so many things to do, once they've finished their homework! Sometimes that takes quite a while.

Once a week Kate goes to Brownies, to learn skills such as first aid and swimming. There is also Cubs for boys, but Jack prefers to play sports. In the winter he goes to football practice once a week, and in the summer he swaps his football boots for a cricket bat!

Some evenings the children come home after school and want to be quiet. When they've done their homework, they play on the computer, watch cartoons on the television, read a book, or draw pictures.

When someone has an accident, the main thing is to keep calm.

☞ At Brownies, Kate and her friends practice first aid on a model.

Tonight for supper, the Taylors are eating fish and chips. As well as fish, meat is popular, and Jack's best meal of the week is Sunday lunchtime. The family has delicious roast meat—it can be chicken, lamb, pork, or beef with roast potatoes, vegetables, and lots of gravy!

Most British people have cereal, toast, and tea or coffee for breakfast, but they still enjoy the traditional bacon and eggs, particularly on weekends.

The family always try to eat supper together so they can discuss what they did during the day.

Fish and chips are my favorite supper. But they are rather fattening!

Drink up your milk as well as eating your supper. It's very good for you.

17

Fish and chips are often bought from special shops, as a "takeaway" to eat at home.

The weekend

It's Saturday, which means no school! Because it's the weekend, Jack and Kate's parents don't have to go to work either. That means the family can spend time together.

Please may we have these biscuits? They're delicious!

Mrs. Taylor takes Kate to the supermarket where they buy the next week's shopping. Mrs. Taylor has a list, and Kate fetches everything and puts the goods in the cart. As they're paying for their shopping, Kate spots a friend from school with her mom, so they all go to a café. The two moms drink coffee, but Kate and her friend each have a milkshake.

18

 Many supermarkets now charge customers for plastic bags, so shoppers take their own.

Jack also likes to go shopping with his mom, but only if he's not playing soccer or cricket! When he's got a match, his dad enjoys coming to watch.

There's usually quite a crowd of onlookers to support the team. Mr. Taylor encourages Jack from the sideline and gets even more excited than his son when Jack scores a goal!

19

Sports are very important in the UK, and many matches take place on the weekend. Rugby and cricket are played, but the most popular sport is soccer.

Thousands of fans flock to games, all of them desperately wanting to see their team win! Wembley Stadium is a newly rebuilt sports venue in London.

Come on, United! You've got to win!

Things people do

Around 200 years ago, the United Kingdom became the first country in the world to be industrialized, which means it began to use machines in place of people to make things. Today most people in the UK work in offices and factories, but there is also a proud tradition of farming.

London is one of the most important financial centers in the world. Among other major cities are Glasgow, Edinburgh, Leeds, Manchester, Belfast, Liverpool, Cardiff, and Birmingham.

The variations of climate and soil mean that different types of farming occur in different regions. Sheep and beef cattle are reared on the more remote hills of northwest England, Scotland, and Wales, dairy cows in the milder southwest of England. Crops and cereals are grown in

Weaving in the 19th century

eastern Scotland and southeast England. Fruit also grows well in the warmer climate of the south of England.

Farming

Find out about the Industrial Revolution at en.wikipedia.org/wiki/Industrial_Revolution

Many British-made products are exported around the world. Scotland is famous for its whisky (known as "Scotch"), and in England they use special hops to make a beer called "bitter."

Whisky

Cheeses such as Red Leicester, Cheddar, and Stilton are delicious, and in Cornwall they're very proud of their Cornish pasties—individual pies made of pastry and filled with meat, potato and onion.

Cornish pasty

Fishing is another important industry. Cod, haddock, and mackerel are common in British waters, and fried cod is what Jack likes best with his chips.

In the North Sea, off the northeast coast of Scotland, there are many oil rigs, which pump oil from the seabed and supply it to the United Kingdom. Living on an oil rig can be tough— can you imagine living in the middle of the stormy sea?

Resupplying an oil rig

Visit www.foodfrombritain.com for lots more British foods.

Mr. Taylor is a scientist and Mrs. Taylor works part-time as the receptionist at a medical center. Kate wants to be a nurse when she grows up. Jack wants to be a fighter pilot in the Royal Air Force; sometimes he sits in the classroom and daydreams of flying a supersonic jet.

Mr. Taylor at work

Primary school education consists of infant school from four to seven years old, junior school from seven to eleven, and then secondary school from eleven years on. Some pupils leave school at age sixteen, but others stay on, either at the same school or go to a college for sixteen to eighteen years old to study for advanced qualifications. Many then go on to university.

Teaching math

Jack, pay attention to the lesson and stop looking out of the window!

24

Find out about the Royal Air Force at www.raf.mod.uk

Facts about the UK

part three

Did you know?

👍 It took the Pilgrim Fathers two months to sail from England to America on the *Mayflower*.

👍 Legend has it that King Alfred was so busy thinking about how to beat the Danes that he burned some cakes that were cooking in the oven.

👍 Henry VIII executed two of his wives, divorced two more, one died in childbirth, and the sixth, Catherine Parr, outlived him.

👍 In 1976, two Belfast women, Mairead Corrigan and Betty Williams, received the Nobel Peace Prize for their Northern Irish peace effort.

👍 Bones found in east England show prehistoric man lived there 700,000 years ago.

👍 In 1783 William Pitt was elected prime minister, at age 24.

👍 The word Wales comes from an Anglo-Saxon word meaning "foreigner."

👍 As well as Hadrian's Wall, the Romans built Gask Ridge and Antonine's Wall to keep the Scots out of England.

👍 The Great Fire of London in 1666 started in a bakery in Pudding Lane.

50 UK history facts

1 3100 B.C. The building of Stonehenge Monument begins on Salisbury Plain, as a circle of timbers.

2 55 B.C. Julius Caesar invades England, but his Roman army is forced to retreat.

Julius Caesar

3 43–77 A.D. The Romans return and conquer first England and then Wales.

4 c.60 A.D. Death of Boudicca, Queen of the Iceni people, who led a major uprising against occupying Roman forces.

Roman soldier

5 122 Hadrian's Wall is built to keep northern tribes out of England.

6 408–450 The Roman army leaves. Britain is attacked by Picts and Saxons.

7 550 St. David brings Christianity to Wales.

8 793 Vikings invade Britain for the first time.

9 924 Athelstan, King of Wessex, defeats alliance of Scots, Celts, and Vikings, and becomes "King of all Britain."

10 1066 King Harold defeats a Norwegian army at Stamford Bridge, but 19 days later is killed at Hastings as the Saxons lose to the Normans led by William the Conqueror.

11 1272–1307 Edward I conquers Wales and later becomes known as the "Hammer of the Scots."

12 1314 The Scots defeat the English at the Battle of Bannockburn and Robert the Bruce declares Scotland independent.

Robert the Bruce

Go to www.battle1066.com to find out more about the Battle of Hastings.

13 **1337–1453** The Hundred Years' War between England and France. Though the English win famous battles at Crécy (1346) and Agincourt (1415), they are finally driven out of France.

14 **1400** Owen Glendower proclaims himself Prince of Wales and then leads a Welsh revolt against the English.

15 **1455–1485** The Wars of the Roses are fought for the English throne. The decisive battle is at Bosworth in 1485 when Richard III is killed and Henry Tudor becomes Henry VII.

16 **1509–1547** Henry VIII reigns as King of England. He breaks away from the Catholic Church and closes 800 monasteries. He rebuilds the English navy.

Henry VIII

17 **1513** A Scottish army invades England and is defeated at Flodden.

18 **1534** The Act of Supremacy, in which Henry VIII establishes himself as supreme head of the Church of England.

19 **1558–1603** The reign of Elizabeth I is notable for the execution of Mary, Queen of Scots (1587), and the defeat of the Spanish Armada (1588).

20 **1605** Catholic plot to kill James I fails and the conspirators, including Guy Fawkes, are executed.

21 **1620** English Puritans, known as the Pilgrim Fathers, set sail in the *Mayflower* and establish a colony in Plymouth, Massachusetts.

Guy Fawkes

22 **1642** Civil War breaks out between the Cavaliers (led by King Charles I) and the Roundheads (led by Oliver Cromwell) when the King tries to arrest five members of parliament. The Roundheads win and Charles is executed in 1649.

23 **1649–60** Cromwell governs England as a republic until his death in 1658. Two years later Charles II is crowned king.

The *Mayflower*

Find out more about Henry VIII at www.brims.co.uk/tudors

24 **1665** The Great Plague kills about 100,000 people in Britain and the next year the Great Fire destroys much of London.

The Great Fire of London

25 **1688** The Glorious Revolution occurs when the Catholic King James II is deposed and the Protestant William of Orange is crowned William III.

26 **1706–1707** The Acts of Union unite the kingdoms of England and Scotland.

27 **1745–46** Jacobite Rebellion in Scotland led by "Bonnie Prince Charlie" ends in the bloody Battle of Culloden.

28 **1769** James Watt's improvements to Newcomen's engine put Britain at the forefront of the Industrial Revolution.

29 **1775–1783** Britain fights and loses the American War of Independence. The Treaty of Paris in 1783 gives the United States its freedom.

30 **1805** The Battle of Trafalgar is fought between Britain and the combined fleets of Spain and France.

31 **1833** The Slavery Abolition Act abolishes slavery throughout the British Empire.

32 **1851** Great Exhibition held in London as a celebration of modern industrial technology.

33 **1854** The Charge of the Light Brigade during the Crimean War is a disaster for a British cavalry brigade.

34 **1901** Queen Victoria dies after a reign of 64 years.

The James Watt Steam Engine

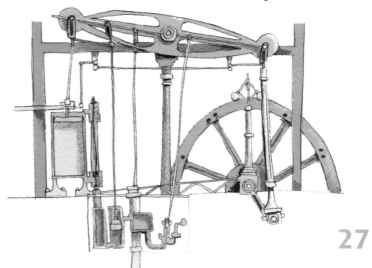

27

Newcomen's steam-powered engine was used to pump water from coal mines. ☞

35 **1914–1918** Britain and her allies defeat Germany in World War I but lose over two million soldiers during four years of bloody fighting.

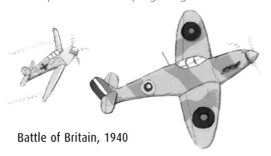

Battle of Britain, 1940

36 **1920** The Anglo-Irish Treaty results in the Irish Free State but the six provinces of Northern Ireland remain within the UK.

37 **1939–1945** Britain declares war on Germany in 1939 and in 1940 stands alone as Hitler conquers Western Europe. In 1941 the USA and Russia join with Britain in the fight against Germany and also Japan, who both surrender in 1945.

38 **1952** King George VI dies and is succeeded by his daughter, Queen Elizabeth II.

39 **1952** The British Comet becomes the world's first jet airliner to carry fare-paying passengers.

40 **1953** A British-led expedition conquers Mt. Everest.

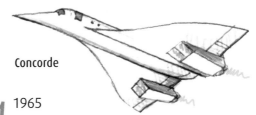

Concorde

41 **1965** Winston Churchill dies.

42 **1966** England wins the soccer World Cup, defeating Germany.

43 **1973** Britain joins the European Economic Community (EEC).

44 **1976** The Anglo-French supersonic airliner, Concorde, makes its first commercial flight.

Margaret Thatcher

45 **1979** Margaret Thatcher becomes Britain's first woman prime minister.

46 **1987** A freak hurricane leaves a trail of devastation over southern England.

47 **1994** The Channel Tunnel opens, linking Britain to France.

48 **1997** Diana, Princess of Wales, dies in a car crash in Paris.

49 **1998** Wales, Scotland, and Northern Ireland establish their own Assemblies.

50 **2007** The famous sailing tea clipper, the *Cutty Sark*, is badly damaged by fire at Greenwich on the River Thames in London.

Brilliant Britons

Leaders

Oliver Cromwell (1599–1658) A brilliant soldier, his Roundhead army defeated King Charles I and turned Britain into a republic for 11 years.

William Gladstone (1809–1898) Was prime minister four times. He wanted home rule for Ireland.

David Lloyd George (1864–1945) The Welsh prime minister who led Britain during WWI and was Britain's delegate at the Paris Peace Conference in 1919.

Winston Churchill (1874–1965) Writer, soldier, and prime minister, Churchill inspired Britain during WWII.

Winston Churchill

Margaret Thatcher (1925–) Britain's first female prime minister who held office for 11 years.

Kings and queens

Alfred the Great (849–899) King of the Anglo-Saxons, he successfully defended England against the Vikings.

Robert the Bruce (1274–1329) Crowned King of the Scots in 1306, he defeated the English army at Bannockburn in 1314.

Henry V (1387–1422) A great king and soldier whose army beat the French at Agincourt in 1415.

Henry VIII (1491–1547) Married six times, he founded the Church of England in 1534.

Elizabeth I (1533–1603) England grew strong during her reign and defeated the Spanish Armada in 1588.

Elizabeth I

Victoria (1819–1901) Became queen at 18 and ruled for 64 years over the British Empire.

Elizabeth II (1926–) Queen since 1952, she has reigned through great social changes in the UK.

Search the internet to discover how a spider helped Robert the Bruce.

Explorers, soldiers, and sportsmen

Francis Drake (c.1540–c.1596) First Englishman to circumnavigate the world.

Captain Cook (1728–1779) Explorer who discovered Australia.

Lord Nelson (1758–1805) Led the British navy to victory against France at the Battle of Trafalgar in 1805.

Duke of Wellington (1769–1852) General who defeated Napoleon at Waterloo in 1815.

Captain Scott (1868–1912) Explorer who reached the South Pole in 1912 but died on the return trip in atrocious conditions.

Field-Marshal Montgomery (1887–1976) Commanded British forces in WWII.

W. G. Grace (1848–1915) Cricketer who dominated the sport in the 19th century.

Bobby Moore (1941–1993) Captained England to victory in the 1966 soccer World Cup final.

Stephen Redgrave (1962–) Won gold medals for rowing in five Olympics.

Bobby Moore

Scientists and inventors

Isaac Newton (1642–1727) English scientist who discovered the laws of gravity and established the Three Laws of Motion.

Isambard Kingdom Brunel (1806–1859) Engineer responsible for pioneering tunnels, railways, steamships, and bridges.

Charles Darwin (1809–1882) Scientist whose theory of natural selection explained the process of evolution.

Sir Isaac Newton

Alexander Fleming (1881–1955) Nobel prizewinner who in 1928 discovered penicillin, used to treat infections.

John Logie Baird (1888–1946) Pioneer in television development who transmitted the first TV pictures in 1925.

Frank Whittle (1907–1996) RAF officer whose ideas on jet propulsion led to the invention of the jet engine.

Francis Crick (1916–2004) Jointly awarded a Nobel Prize for discovering the structure of DNA in 1953.

Tim Berners-Lee (1955–) Invented the World Wide Web in 1989.

Visit www.show.me.uk to find out about science, technology, and more!

Writers

William Shakespeare

(1564–1616) Poet and playwright whose works such as *Romeo and Juliet*, *Hamlet*, and *Macbeth* are still staged worldwide.

Shakespeare

Jane Austen (1775–1817)

Writer of novels such as *Pride and Prejudice* which describe the lives of English women in the 19th century.

Charles Dickens (1812–1870) Writer

whose novels such as *Oliver Twist* and *Great Expectations* provide vivid accounts of Victorian life.

Charlotte Brontë (1816–1855) The eldest

of three sisters who were all novelists, Charlotte is best remembered for *Jane Eyre*, while Emily Brontë's *Wuthering Heights* remains a classic.

Arthur Conan Doyle

(1859–1930) Graduating first as a doctor, he became a writer, best known for creating Sherlock Holmes.

J. M. Barrie (1860–1937) Playwright and

children's author famous for his character Peter Pan, the boy who wouldn't grow up. Royalties from performances of the play were left to the Great Ormond Street Hospital for Children in London.

Rudyard Kipling

(1865–1936) Writer of stories, poems, and the children's classic, *Jungle Book*.

Agatha Christie

(1890–1976) Creator of detective stories featuring Miss Marple and Hercule Poirot.

Charlotte Brontë

J. R. R. Tolkien (1892–1973) Tolkien fought

in WWI and wrote *The Hobbit* and *The Lord of the Rings* while a professor at Oxford University.

Enid Blyton (1897–1968) Wrote over 700

children's books and created the Famous Five and the Secret Seven.

J. K. Rowling (1965–) Wrote her first Harry

Potter story in 1995. The incredibly popular books have been translated into 65 different languages and turned into very successful movies.

Oliver Twist

31

Actors and entertainers

Charlie Chaplin (1889–1977) London-born actor and comedian who was an early Hollywood star with his "Tramp" character.

Stan Laurel (1890–1965) English-born actor who moved to the U.S. and found fame with Oliver Hardy.

Alfred Hitchcock (1899–1980) Film director/producer best known for suspense films such as *Rear Window*.

Charlie Chaplin

Sir Laurence Olivier (1907–1989) Brilliant on stage and screen, Olivier won two Oscars and many other acting awards.

Dame Vera Lynn (1917–) Entertainer known as the "Forces' Sweetheart" because of the songs she sang to British troops during World War ll.

The Beatles The four-man band from Liverpool were worldwide superstars in the 1960s with songs such as *She Loves You* and *I Want to Hold Your Hand*.

Rolling Stones Formed in 1961, the Stones are still playing and lead singer Mick Jagger was knighted in 2003.

Dame Judi Dench (1934–) Award-winning actress who plays "M" in the James Bond movies and won an Oscar for her role as Elizabeth I in *Shakespeare in Love*.

Sir Ian McKellen (1939–) Shakespearean stage and screen actor who played Gandalf in the film *Lord of the Rings*.

David Bowie (1947–) Singer best known for songs such as *Heroes* and *Ziggy Stardust*. He has sold nearly 200 million albums.

Sacha Baron Cohen (1971–) Golden Globe winning actor who invented the comic characters Ali G and Borat.

David Bowie

Vera Lynn

Do some detective work to discover the name of Sherlock Holmes' doctor friend.

Things to see

LONDON

Big Ben The world's largest four-faced chiming clock, Big Ben is part of the Houses of Parliament and started to operate in 1859.

London Eye Nearly four million people each year take a spin on the Eye (also known as the Millennium Wheel). The wheel, (443 ft. high) is by the Thames and gives wonderful views of London.

Westminster Abbey Built 1,000 years ago, the Abbey is traditionally where monarchs are crowned and buried.

Buckingham Palace The official London residence of the Royal Family since 1837, it has 775 rooms and a series of paintings called the Royal Collection.

National Gallery Opened in 1824, the gallery in Trafalgar Square has one of the greatest collections of European paintings in the world.

Madame Tussauds The famous wax museum was opened in 1884 and features famous historical and royal figures plus murderers, film and sports stars.

Hampton Court Palace Became a royal palace during the reign of Henry VIII, around 1525. It has a maze with half a mile of paths.

Tower of London Built on the Thames by William the Conqueror in 1078 to protect London, it has been a prison and a place of execution. The crown jewels are now kept here.

Houses of Parliament Also known as the Palace of Westminster, it is the home of the English Parliament.

Tower Bridge The bridge, which took eight years to build, was opened in 1894. It lifts in the middle to allow ships to sail up the River Thames.

Tower Bridge

Visit www.madametussauds.com/London to discover the latest wax models.

ENGLAND

Stonehenge The most important pre-historic monument in Britain, this collection of earthworks and standing stones dates back to around 3100 B.C. No one knows who built Stonehenge or why.

Windsor Castle One of the Royal Family's official residences, it is the largest occupied castle in the world and was built nearly 1,000 years ago by William the Conqueror.

Roman Baths Two thousand years after they were built, the Roman baths (for which the city of Bath is named) attract one million visitors each year.

Stratford-upon-Avon The birthplace of William Shakespeare, it's possible to visit several properties connected with him. The Royal Shakespeare Company performs here.

Leeds Castle This Kent castle was built in 1119 by a Norman knight and became a royal palace. Elizabeth I was briefly imprisoned here.

Sherwood Forest Legendary home of Robin Hood and his Merry Men, this historic royal hunting forest is now a country park and open to the public.

Hadrian's Wall Named after the Roman Emperor Hadrian, the 73-mile wall was begun in 122 A.D. It was built across the north of England to keep out the Picts.

Oxford Known as the City of Dreaming Spires because of its beautiful buildings, Oxford is home to Britain's oldest university.

Lake District A region of great natural beauty in the north of England, the Lake District contains Scafell Pike (3,200 ft.), the highest mountain in England.

Roman baths

Will Scarlet and Little John were friends of which famous English outlaw?

SCOTLAND

Edinburgh Castle An ancient fortress, the castle dominates the city and houses the oldest surviving building in Edinburgh. Since 1861, the One O'Clock Gun has been fired at 1 P.M. (except Sundays).

Stone of Destiny Housed in the Edinburgh Castle, the Stone is also known as the Stone of Scone, on which Scottish kings sat when they were crowned 1,000 years ago.

Greyfriars Bobby The statue of the Skye Terrier dog celebrates the loyal friend of a 19th-century Edinburgh man.

Kelvingrove Art Gallery and Museum This imposing red sandstone building in Glasgow contains a huge range of artifacts including paintings, sculptures and fossils.

The Royal Yacht Britannia Permanently moored at Leith, near Edinburgh, the 410-foot long yacht used to belong to the Royal Family and sailed more than one million nautical miles before being retired.

Ben Nevis In the far north of Scotland, this mountain is 4,406 feet high and is popular with walkers and rock climbers.

Loch Ness Famed for its monster (which has yet to be caught!), Loch Ness is 24 miles long and 754 feet deep.

St. Andrews University town by the sea, known as the Home of Golf. The British Open Golf Championship is often played here.

Forth Rail Bridge This landmark bridge straddles the Firth of Forth. It is 1.5 miles long and was built in the 1880s.

Greyfriars
Bobby

Loch Ness

Plan a visit to the Royal Yacht at www.royalyachtbritannia.co.uk

NORTHERN IRELAND

Giant's Causeway The result of an ancient volcanic eruption, the Giant's Causeway is a series of rock columns on the northeast coast of Northern Ireland. Legend has it the columns were used as stepping stones by a giant so he could walk to Scotland.

Carrickfergus Castle A Norman castle on Belfast Lough, this well-preserved fortress was besieged many times in its history.

Carrickfergus Castle

Belfast Botanic Gardens The stunning Gardens opened in 1828 and the most popular feature is the Palm House containing many rare plants.

Ulster Folk and Transport Museum This fascinating museum near Belfast gives an insight into the way of life and traditions of the people of the North of Ireland.

WALES

Tintern Abbey Built around 1130 alongside the River Wye, Tintern Abbey was for centuries the home of monks until destroyed by King Henry VIII.

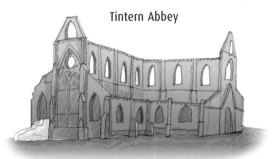

Tintern Abbey

Snowdonia National Park This beautiful region in North Wales contains forests, lakes, and Mt. Snowdon. A mountain railway takes visitors to the top.

Gower Peninsula On the Welsh south coast, the peninsula has beautiful beaches, caves, castles, and coves.

Caernarfon Castle 13th-century castle where the Queen crowned Prince Charles Prince of Wales in 1969.

Portmeirion A spectacular Italianate village in North Wales begun in the 1920s.

Harlech Castle Building begun in 1283 for King Edward I of England during his war with the Welsh. In the 15th century, the castle was besieged for seven years.

Go to www.eryri-npa.co.uk/ to see spectacular views of Snowdonia.

50 facts about the UK

1 Berwick upon Tweed, the northernmost town in England, has changed hands between England and Scotland many times.

2 The giant liner, *Titanic*, was launched in Belfast in 1911.

3 On Remembrance Day in November, poppies are worn to commemorate the soldiers killed in war.

Wearing a poppy

4 Policemen in the UK don't carry guns on standard patrol.

5 The last battle to be fought on British soil was the Battle of Culloden in 1746, when the English beat the Scots.

6 The longest cable car ride in the UK is in Llandudno in North Wales.

7 On January 25, the Scots celebrate Burns Night, the anniversary of the birth of poet Robert Burns in 1759.

8 December 26 is called Boxing Day because in olden days workers were given a Christmas box filled with money.

9 Public holidays in the UK are called Bank Holidays because on these days banks are closed.

10 The North American name for a bowler hat comes from the British Earl of Derby, who died in 1834.

11 Shrove Tuesday, also known as Pancake Day, falls on the day before Ash Wednesday, the first day of Lent.

Flipping a pancake

12 David Beckham, the soccer star, is married to Victoria, "Posh Spice" of the pop group, the Spice Girls.

13 Scotland soccer fans are known as the Tartan Army because they often go to matches wearing their kilts.

The *Titanic*

Find out about the Battle of Culloden at www.britishbattles.com

14 The sandwich was named after the Fourth Earl of Sandwich who died in 1792.

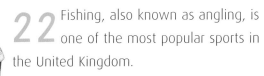

Earl of Sandwich

15 In 1954, Roger Bannister was the first man to run a mile in under four minutes.

16 The oldest soccer club in the world is Sheffield FC, which was founded in 1857.

17 The oldest tennis tournament in the world is the Wimbledon Championships, which were first held in 1877.

18 Arthur Wynne, a journalist from Liverpool, invented the crossword puzzle in 1913.

19 Briton William Bourne is credited with first coming up with the idea of a submarine, back in 1578.

20 John McAdam was a Scot who, in the 1820s, invented a process for building roads with a smooth hard surface.

21 The first bicycle with foot pedals was invented by a Scot, Kirkpatrick Macmillan, in the 1830s.

22 Fishing, also known as angling, is one of the most popular sports in the United Kingdom.

23 The Lord Mayor's show takes place on the second Saturday in November, when the Mayor of the City of London swears allegiance to the Queen.

24 The highest recorded temperature in the UK was 38.5°C (101.3°F) in Kent in August 2003.

25 The UK was the first country to introduce adhesive postage stamps in 1840. They were invented by James Chalmers.

26 The United Kingdom is a constitutional monarchy with the Queen as Head of State.

Penny Black stamps

27 Nearly 30 million tourists visit the United Kingdom each year.

Fishing

38

28 Heathrow Airport in London is the busiest airport in the world and handles about 63 million passengers each year.

29 Author J. K. Rowling wrote parts of her first Harry Potter book in a café in Edinburgh while out of work.

30 The 2012 Summer Olympics will be held in London.

31 The last Olympics to be hosted in the UK were the 1948 London Games.

32 A painting by Lucian Freud broke the world auction record for a work by a living artist when it sold for 30 million dollars in New York in May, 2008.

33 The ceremonial guardians of the Crown Jewels in the Tower of London are better known as Beefeaters.

34 The London Underground train system first ran in 1863 and is the oldest of its kind in the world.

35 The Channel Tunnel rail link between England and France is 31 miles long and opened in 1994.

A Beefeater

36 Sir James Dewar invented the vacuum flask in 1892.

37 Anglesey, off the northwest coast of Wales, is the largest Welsh island and covers 276 square miles.

38 Lewis Carroll, the author of *Alice's Adventures in Wonderland* was christened Charles Lutwidge Dodgson.

London Underground

39

39 The London to Brighton Veteran Car Run takes place on the first Sunday in November.

40 Nearly two million children were evacuated from cities to the countryside during World War II to protect them from German bombing raids.

Catherine of Braganza

41 Tea first became popular in the UK in the 1660s when King Charles II married the Portuguese princess, Catherine of Braganza, who brought tea in her dowry.

42 Florence Nightingale, also known as the Lady of the Lamp, was a British nurse who improved the welfare of soldiers during the Crimean War in the 1850s.

43 *Danny Boy*, the popular song set to the Irish tune *Londonderry Air*, was actually written by an Englishman.

44 Tradition has it that anyone born within the sound of the bells of St. Mary-le-Bow Church in East London is called a Cockney.

45 Jack the Ripper was the name given to an unidentified murderer who killed five London women in the late 19th century but was never caught.

46 The legendary sword said to belong to King Arthur was called Excalibur.

Excalibur

47 The Beatles have had more number-one singles in the UK charts than any other British artist.

48 The first superhighway in England was opened in 1958.

49 Seventy percent of people in the UK speak only English and no other language.

50 *The Book of Household Management* compiled by Mrs. Beeton was published in 1861 and was an instant best seller.

Florence Nightingale

40

Search the internet to discover what kind of table King Arthur had!

Have a nice day in the UK!

Join me on an exciting trip to Snowdonia National Park in Wales.

part four

Did you know?

👍 Once a year there are cheese rolling races in England when scores of people race down a steep slope after a special cheese.

👍 The Bank of England has issued banknotes since 1694.

👍 The earliest known sighting of the Loch Ness Monster was in 565 by St. Columba.

👍 The official taxis in London are known as "Black Cabs."

👍 Rubens' masterpiece *The Adoration of the Magi* is in King's College Chapel, Cambridge.

👍 The Wellington boot is named after the Duke of Wellington, the general who defeated Napoleon at the Battle of Waterloo.

👍 The Millennium Dome in London is the largest domed structure in the world. It is now called The O2 and is used for pop concerts.

👍 The Isle of Man is not part of the UK but is a Crown dependency with its own laws, courts, and government.

👍 The Royal Family likes to spend summer in Balmoral, a beautiful castle in the Scottish Highlands bought by Queen Victoria in 1848.

👍 71 percent of British people are Christian; Buddhism, Islam, Hinduism, Judaism, and Sikhism are also practiced.

All the accents

It's great fun traveling around the United Kingdom. Not only are there lots of things to see and do, but you'll hear lots of different accents— some British regional accents and many from overseas!

Dialects and accents are quite difficult to understand in some regions of the UK, even for British people who are visiting towns or villages far from their own locality. The vocabulary also varies by region and you may already know that British people have different words than Americans for familiar objects. For example, a cookie is a biscuit in the UK, a Band-Aid is a plaster, and garbage is rubbish!

British people often talk about the weather when they meet.

There are many multicultural communities in the UK. In the 1950s and 1960s lots of people came from the British Commonwealth. More recently, when membership of the European Community became bigger, many Europeans, particularly from Eastern Europe, have come to Britain to live and work.

Good morning. Isn't it cold today?

Yes, but at least the sun is shining.

41

Let's go to London

It's holiday time and the Taylor family are off to visit their friends and family around the UK. First they drive to London. Jack and Kate can hardly contain their excitement as they see the signposts to the capital!

*Oh look!
There's one of
the famous ravens!*

Jack and Kate have never been to London before and the first thing they want to do is visit the Tower of London where the Crown Jewels are kept. Legend has it that Britain will cease to be a powerful nation if the ravens leave the Tower, so you will always be able to see one there. The man in uniform is called a Beefeater.

The Tower of London

42

Cleopatra's Needle

Tower Bridge

The "Gherkin" building

After visiting the Tower, the Taylors take a sightseeing boat trip up the River Thames. A guide points out famous landmarks such as Tower Bridge, Cleopatra's Needle, and the Houses of Parliament. What an exhausting day! Everyone is hungry when they disembark, and they head to a burger bar for cheeseburgers and milkshakes.

London is a really great city! There's so much to do here.

Yes. And people come from all over the world just to see it for themselves.

43

The "Gherkin" is the second tallest building in the City of London.

Trooping the Color

June is a wonderful time to be in London. There is the chance to see the Queen! Each June the British army parades before the Queen in a ceremony called Trooping the Color. It is also the Queen's official birthday.

Those tall hats that they're wearing are made of bearskin.

The cricket match

Jack's a real cricket fan so he wants to go to Lord's to see a match.

Cricket is the summer sport in the United Kingdom and it's played between April and September. Some matches can last five days, and even after all that time, the match may finish in a draw!

Lord's Cricket Ground in London is called the Home of Cricket and cricket was first played here in 1814. Each team has eleven players.

Oh, great shot! The fielder will have to chase that one!

That's going for four runs. The other side must be getting worried now!

Both teams wear white clothes. The rules of cricket are quite complicated, but basically one team is trying to score more runs than the other team. The batsmen do this by hitting the ball as far as they can. But for many people it's not important who wins the match! The beauty of cricket is the peaceful atmosphere. You can watch the game with a nice cup of tea and a slice of cake. Then you can take a nap in the sunshine as play continues.

Only 50 more runs to win. I think we'll make it.

It's time the bowler was changed. He's giving away too many runs.

Visiting Stonehenge

The Taylors are heading to Wales to see some relatives, but on their way they stop at Stonehenge to look at the UK's oldest tourist attraction.

Stonehenge dates from around 3100 B.C. when prehistoric men built a bank from shoveled earth. Then, over the next few hundred years, their ancestors erected a series of huge standing stones. Some of the stones are 12 feet high—twice the size of Mr. Taylor! Imagine how hard it must have been to build Stonehenge.

Those stones are awesome. And to think there was no machinery to lift them.

Historians aren't sure exactly what the purpose of Stonehenge was, but the most likely explanation is that it was a place of worship, possibly for honoring the Sun God. Stonehenge is one of the most important prehistoric sites in the world.

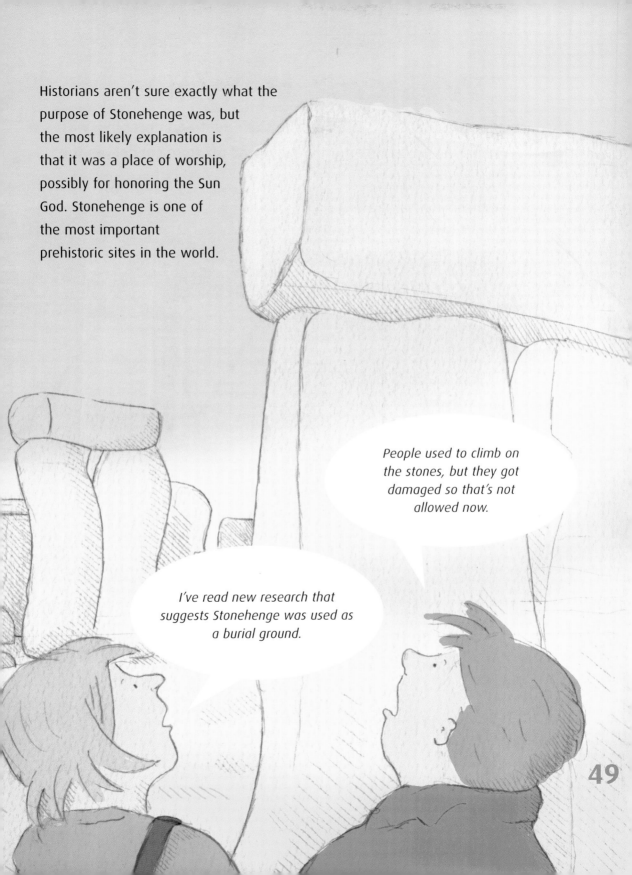

People used to climb on the stones, but they got damaged so that's not allowed now.

I've read new research that suggests Stonehenge was used as a burial ground.

49

Welcome to Wales

Next stop for the Taylors is Wales, where their aunt and uncle live with their two children, Huw and Megan. They head off from London on the M4 for the Severn Bridge.

The Severn Bridge is a mile-long suspension bridge that links England to Wales across the River Severn. It was opened in 1966 by the Queen and since then more than 300 million vehicles have crossed. There is a toll on the bridge, which means that every car has to pay money to go over it.

Once we're over the bridge, it's only 25 miles until we get to Cardiff.

50

 Go to www.visitwales.com for lots of information about what to do in Wales.

Jack and Kate's cousins, Huw and Megan, speak Welsh as well as English, but of course Jack and Kate don't understand Welsh, so when they go to lunch they all speak in English!

How do you say "Good morning" in Welsh?

"Bore da." And "thank-you" is "diolch."

They have lunch in Cardiff Bay, which used to be one of the busiest ports in the UK when coal from the Welsh valleys was exported. Now the Bay is a modern complex full of shops, restaurants, and offices.

Cardiff Bay Opera House

Millennium Center at Cardiff Bay

51

Welsh is one of the oldest spoken languages.

Climbing in Snowdonia

The Taylors leave Cardiff and drive toward Snowdonia National Park in the far north of Wales. It's not long before Jack and Kate can see the top of Mount Snowdon.

Snowdonia National Park is one of the most beautiful regions in the United Kingdom. It covers 823 square miles.

It wasn't difficult to put up the tent. I hope it will keep out any wild animals!

People have lived in this part of Wales for a long time, Jack. I think we'll all be safe!

 Snowdonia was designated a National Park in 1951, followed by two other Welsh areas.

There are lakes, forests, pastures and, of course, there is the 3,560-foot-high Mt. Snowdon, the tallest mountain in Wales. After a night in their tent, the family sets off to climb to the top of Snowdon. Jack is more interested in the mountain railway.

This train goes right to the top of Mt. Snowdon. That's the way for me!

The locomotive pushes the carriage up the mountain

There are lots of other activities in Snowdonia National Park such as biking, canoeing, and rock climbing. There are also unusual species to see: plants such as the Snowdon Lily, and the rainbow leaf beetle, or Snowdon beetle.

Kayaking is different from canoeing, but I think I'm getting the hang of it now!

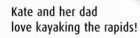

Kate and her dad love kayaking the rapids!

53

The Welsh name for Mt. Snowdon is Yr Wyddfa which means "burial mound."

Visiting Edinburgh Castle

The Taylors have reached Edinburgh, the capital of Scotland, and one of the most beautiful cities in the world.

 The Edinburgh International Festival takes place during August every year.

The next day the family explores Edinburgh, starting with the magnificent castle. There are great views of the city from the ramparts, but watch out for the One O'Clock Gun . . . Bang! The gun is fired each day so the people of Edinburgh can check their watches. Kate's head is ringing now!

After the castle, the Taylors walk down a road called the Royal Mile to the Palace of Holyroodhouse, which is the official residence of the Queen in Scotland. Nearby is Arthur's Seat, a hill which Jack and Kate love to climb for the great views.

The One O'Clock Gun being fired from the castle.

The family is staying with their grandparents. For supper that evening they tuck into plates of haggis, neeps, and tatties . . . delicious! Haggis is sheep meat mixed with onion and oatmeal and then boiled. "Neeps" are turnips and "tatties" means potatoes.

Here you are!
Your favorite
Scottish supper!

55

Edinburgh is the second most visited tourist destination in the United Kingdom.

Hunting Nessie

Lakes in Scotland are called "lochs" and in the north of the country is the most famous loch of all—Loch Ness.

Why is Loch Ness famous? Because of its monster called Nessie! Unfortunately, Nessie is very shy and doesn't like to come to the surface very often. Instead, she prefers to swim about in the deep, dark waters of Loch Ness.

There have been many "sightings" of the Loch Ness Monster, and in the last century some people claimed they had caught Nessie on camera. But the photographs were either blurry or just a practical joke.

Underwater searches of the loch have been done, using powerful lights and cameras, but no trace of Nessie has ever been found. She must have a great hiding place!

Perhaps Nessie looks like this!

I'm going to have my camera ready in case Nessie appears!

I think Nessie might be a dinosaur called plesiosaurus. They lived millions of years ago.

The Giant's Causeway

The Taylors have crossed by ferry from Scotland to Northern Ireland, and they've gone to explore the amazing Giant's Causeway.

The Giant's Causeway is on the northeast coast of Northern Ireland just by the sea. An old legend has it that the blocks were built by an Irish giant called Finn MacCool so he could walk across the Irish Sea to fight a Scottish giant. A causeway is a road built over water, which is why it's called the Giant's Causeway!

I know there's no giant, but it sure looks like someone put these blocks here on purpose!

Hold onto my hand, Jack! The rocks can be a bit slippery when they're wet.

In fact the 40,000 blocks were made thousands of years ago by a volcanic explosion. Some of the blocks are 36 feet high and most are hexagonal-shaped, which means they have six sides. They are great fun to walk on, but be careful—the seawater can make them slippery.

The Giant's Causeway is the most popular tourist destination in Northern Ireland, but there are plenty of other strange objects to see as well as the blocks. Look out for rocks called the Giant's Boot, the Pipe Organ, and the Chimney Stack!

The countryside in Northern Ireland is green and hilly.

Look at those two on the stones! They're really having a great time.

I still remember the first time I visited here—we drove over from Londonderry on the way to Belfast.

Bonfire Night

The summer is over and the Taylors are back home. It's November 5, which is a special day in the UK called Bonfire Night. All over the country bonfires blaze, fireworks bang, and boys and girls jump up and down with excitement as people remember Guy Fawkes.

So who was Guy Fawkes? Well, in 1605 a group of men plotted to blow up the Houses of Parliament while King James I of England was giving a speech on November 5. They didn't like the king and wanted him dead.

The plotters rented a cellar under the Houses of Parliament and filled it with barrels of gunpowder, but on the night of November 4 the cellars were searched by suspicious soldiers and Guy Fawkes was caught. Fawkes and the other plotters were executed and the country celebrated the King's escape from death by burning a dummy of Guy Fawkes on a bonfire.

More than 400 years later poor old Guy Fawkes is still burned every November 5 on bonfires all over the country!

Guy Fawkes is discovered.

There's the traitor! Arrest him at once.

 Children make their own dummies of Guy Fawkes and call out "a penny for the guy."

Find out more about Guy Fawkes at www.bonfirenight.net

Clothes

Although British and Americans speak the same language, some words are different, which can be confusing at times! Jack and Kate are wearing clothes that might be called one thing in the UK and another in the United States. Watch out! "Pants" in the UK are girls' underwear!

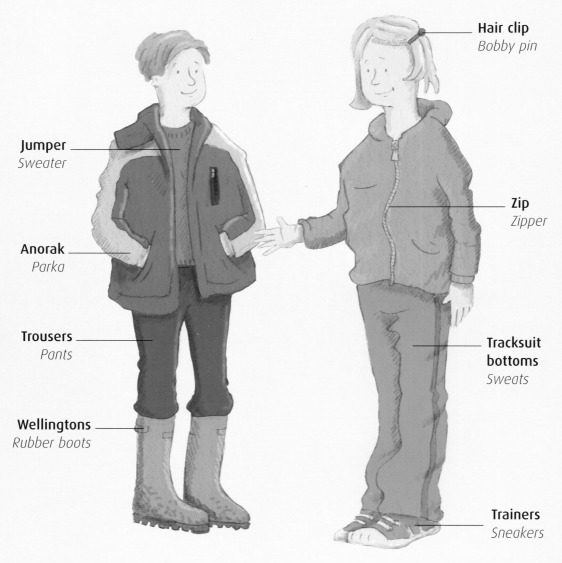

Hair clip
Bobby pin

Jumper
Sweater

Zip
Zipper

Anorak
Parka

Trousers
Pants

Tracksuit
bottoms
Sweats

Wellingtons
Rubber boots

Trainers
Sneakers

Check out lots more different words at www.miketodd.net/encyc/lingo/htm

Weights and measures

When it comes to weighing and measuring things in the UK you need to remember something quite important—although the British use meters and kilograms (the metric system), many people also still use yards and pounds (the imperial system). But read on—all will be explained!

Measures of weight

One ounce = 28.35 grams

One pound = 453.6 grams

One stone = 6.35 kilograms

One ton = 1,016 kilograms

Wow! I've grown nearly five centimeters since I last measured myself!

Measures of volume

One fluid ounce = 28.41 milliliters

One pint = 568.2 milliliters

One gallon = 4.546 liters

We'll be as tall as Mom and Dad soon!

Measures of length

One inch = 2.54 centimeters

One foot = 0.304 meters

One mile = 1,609 meters

63

There are one hundred centimeters in one meter.

Pounds and pence

In 2002 the euro became the official currency of Europe, except in the United Kingdom. The British were so proud of their own currency, they refused to change! So while you buy things in euros in Europe, in the UK it's still pounds (£) and pence (p). 100 pence equals 1 pound.

The Queen's face is always on one side of British banknotes, but on the other is a famous face from the past, such as Charles Dickens. Next time you get your hands on a banknote have a look to see who's on yours!

Although pounds and pence are used in Scotland, their banknotes are different from the rest of the UK.

Acknowledgments

First edition for the United States and Canada published in 2009 by Barron's Educational Series, Inc., Hauppauge, USA.

© 2009 Tony Potter Publishing Ltd., West Sussex, England

www.tonypotter.com

Written by **Gavin Mortimer**
Designed by **Andrea Slane**
Illustrated by **Tim Hutchinson**

All inquiries should be addressed to:
Barron's Educational Series, Inc.
250 Wireless Blvd.
Hauppauge, NY 11788
www.barronseduc.com

ISBN-13: 978-0-7641-6168-1
ISBN-10: 0-7641-6168-7
Library of Congress Control Number: 2008930810

Printed in China

9 8 7 6 5 4 3 2 1

 The pound is 1,200 years old, dating from about 775 A.D.